BECOMING ME
TO BECOME HER

ISBN:
Paperback: 978-1-9633060-3-3

Cover Design: Marquita Desire'e
Interior Design: Marquita Desire'e
Publisher: Self-published by Marquita Desire'e
Printed in the United States of America

This book is a work of nonfiction based on personal
experience. Events, conversations, and timelines are
presented to the best of the author's memory.

The Breaking That Became My Becoming

Dedication

Alexander and Makynlee
you are my reason for pressing on when giving up felt easier. Your unconditional love is my anchor, my grounding force, and the constant reminder that I am never walking this journey alone.

Momma, Grannie, and Cedrick
thank you for always having my back, for your prayers, your example, and your love that has carried me farther than you know.

Sherice Nicole
thank you for seeing me. Your belief in me gives me courage, your encouragement sparks action, and your words remind me that becoming is a journey worth taking.

Stanley Freeman
thank you for showing up , for covering me in prayer, for standing with me when life feels heavy, and for being a steady voice of reason and calm. Your loyalty, compassion, and genuine support have been a gift I do not take lightly.

Marquitta Denise, Tameria, Forrest, Tressa, Lamont, Trinita, Angel, Angela, Sheena, Pastor G. Warren , Darius McClain, Jill, Aharia, Ryan, Carla, Avis, Menasha, Yvette, Chali,
and those I haven't named,
Thank you for the kindness, support, and quiet strength you pour into me along the way.

PROLOGUE

Before you turn the page, let me say this from my heart.
I am sharing parts of my journey not for pity or judgment,
but so someone else can learn from the mistakes I made and
the truth I had to face. These pages come from real places in
my life. Places where I was hurting, confused, hopeful, afraid,
and growing all at the same time.

There was a season when I forgot I was that girl. I dimmed my
own light. I questioned my worth. I stayed in places that
drained me because I believed holding on made me strong. I
ignored what I felt, accepted less than I deserved, and tried to
fix things that were never my assignment. You will see those
moments here. The times I settled. The times I gave too
much. The times I lost myself trying to become what others
needed me to be.

But you will also see my strength rising. You will see my
healing taking shape. You will see the woman I am becoming
as I learn to choose myself, honor my truth, and stand in the
identity I once abandoned.

This is not a story of blame. Yes, people mishandled me. Yes,
some took advantage of my heart. But I also stayed too long. I
tolerated too much. I played small when God created me to
stand tall. This is me owning my part while refusing to be
silent about what I lived through.

I am telling my truth, not to tear anyone down, but to build
something in you. If my honesty helps you remember who
you are, walk away from what is hurting you, forgive yourself,
or rise with new strength, then every word on these pages
was worth writing.

As you read, I hope you feel seen. I hope you feel understood.
And I hope you feel permission to grow, to heal, and to
become the woman you were always meant to be.

Here is to healing out loud.

Here is to becoming her.

Love you, girl.
Marquita Desiree

BECOMING ME TO BECOME HER

TABLE OF CONTENTS

SECTION ONE

THE BECOMING
BEFORE THE BECOMING

1

When Love Was the Goal

In my twenties, I wasn't chasing purpose. I was chasing belonging. I didn't know who I was; I only knew who I wanted to be to someone. If love were a classroom, I would be the student who never missed a day but kept failing every test.

I wanted to be chosen so badly that I confused attention for affection and possession for protection. Every man felt like a maybe. Maybe he'd be different. Maybe he'd finally see me. Maybe this time I could stop proving I was worth loving.

When I look back on that girl at twenty, full of light, she was beautiful. Not just pretty, but radiant. She was talented, creative, and bold enough to believe she could take on the world. I had dreams bigger than my surroundings. I wanted to be on stages and in lights, using my voice to touch hearts. I saw myself in Hollywood, in music, in movement. I was a walking possibility.

But somewhere along the way, that light started to dim. Not because I wanted it to, but because every time I began to shine, someone nearby felt the need to remind me not to glow too brightly. "Be humble," they'd say. "Don't act like you all that." I didn't realize it then, but those small cuts of comparison and criticism were carving away at my confidence one piece at a time.

I learned early that some people mistake confidence for arrogance and joy for showing off. And because I wanted to be liked, I started to shrink. I laughed softer, dreamed smaller, and took up less space. I told myself I was staying humble, but really, I was slowly disappearing.

I was bubbly, friendly, and full of hope, but I also started second-guessing everything that made me who I was. Somewhere between trying to keep people comfortable and trying to be accepted, I started believing the lie that I had to earn my right to shine.

By the time love entered the picture, I was already running on empty. I didn't realize that the version of me showing up for relationships had been chipped away long before love ever hurt me. Not by heartbreak, but by the subtle messages that told me I was too much. Too confident. Too friendly. Too seen.

So when I met men who made me feel seen, even if it was temporary and came with conditions, I mistook that momentary validation for worth.

Back then, I called it loyalty. Now I know it was fear. Fear of being alone. Fear of being forgotten. Fear that without someone to love me, I didn't matter.

Looking back, I can see the girl I was: eager, passionate, naïve, and hungry for stability. She didn't need saving; she needed grounding. But she didn't know that. She only knew survival.

So she played the part. She smiled when it hurt. She forgave when she should have fled. She kept choosing potential over peace, endurance over wisdom, and chaos over clarity because chaos felt familiar.

No one told her that being ride-or-die meant she would spend years dying for people who never even planned to ride.

If I could talk to that girl now, I'd tell her: You weren't crazy, you were craving consistency. You weren't weak; you were worn out. You weren't too much, you were just misplaced. But I didn't know that yet. Back then, all I knew was how to keep trying, keep proving, and keep giving pieces of myself away in exchange for moments that looked like love. And that's where my story begins, with a woman who wanted to be loved so badly that she mistook struggle for devotion. Before I ever learned how to stand alone, I learned how to hold somebody down. I called it love. I called it loyalty. But really, it was survival dressed up as commitment. And that's how I met him, the man who would test every definition of ride-or-die I ever believed in.

2

The Do-or-Die Chick That Had to Die

Loyal to a Lie

I used to believe loyalty could fix anything. If I held a man down long enough, maybe he would finally see my worth. But the truth is, sometimes holding him down means you are sinking with him.

I met him through a mutual friend, and the chemistry was instant. He had the looks, the swag, and said all the right things. He moved with intention. I told myself I was going to take it slow, but I was already gone. It felt real. Real enough for me to forget my common sense.

And not just my common sense... my foundation.

The things I was raised to believe, the values my mama and grandmama drilled into me about self-respect, discernment, and protecting my peace. I pushed all of that to the side. There were certain things you didn't do with a man before marriage, certain lines you didn't cross, and I knew better. But knowing better doesn't always mean doing better. Somewhere between wanting to be chosen and not wanting to be alone, I let go of the woman I was raised to be and picked up someone I barely recognized.

My granny always says, "Don't trust a wooden nickel."
Back then, I really didn't get it. Whew. I should have
listened, because baby... I trusted one, and it cost me
more than money ever could.

Before I knew it, I was all in, heart, hope, and half the
rent.

Two weeks later, yes, you read that correctly, I moved in
with him. I didn't move into a house. I didn't move into
an apartment. I moved into a hotel room with a man I
barely knew. That should have told me everything I
needed to know. But back then, I was so blinded by the
idea of "we" that I ignored the reality of where. It wasn't
stability; it was survival disguised as love. I called it
starting fresh, but really, it was starting over in a
struggle with someone who didn't even belong in my
future.

We got a room at an extended-stay hotel, half-and-half
on the rent, like we were building something. I called it a
partnership, but it was desperation and a dumb decision.
I left stability for struggle, chasing a man.

Before we ever moved in, I had seen him at a party. A
woman caught me scoping him out, so she came up to
me, said hello, and claimed her territory. She pointed at
him and said, "Yeah, that's my man," while rubbing her
pregnant belly. When I asked him later about their
relationship and her being pregnant, he acted shocked,
like he didn't know she was expecting at all. He said they
used to talk, but didn't anymore. I chose to believe him
because believing him felt better than believing her.

At first, life in that tiny room felt like love. He made me laugh, we had great conversations, and I felt like he had my back. We had a routine that ran like clockwork. Certain days, I would drop him off at work and pick him up, and certain days I would let him drop me off and take my car so he could run errands. I was sure he didn't have time to entertain anyone else. Our relationship wasn't defined as a couple, but we did everything couples do. So for me, that was good enough.

As time went on, I started noticing that every morning he would turn his back and start typing on his phone, fingers moving quietly and steady. When I asked who he was texting, he would grin and say, "Nobody, babe. Go back to sleep." And I would because I wanted peace more than I wanted truth.

Some people's peace is just performance. They're calm because they've mastered the art of hiding chaos.

Then came the day he rushed in, breathless, saying his friend had been in a bad car accident. "It's bad," he said, grabbing a jacket. "He might not make it." My heart clenched. I drove him to the hospital, praying the whole way, and dropped him off. He promised to call me soon.

He didn't.

Two days passed... silence. When I told my girlfriend at work, she side-eyed me. "Girl, that doesn't sound like a car accident. That sounds like somebody having a baby."

I laughed it off, but her words sat heavy on my chest.

Weeks went by. The laughter in our room got quieter. My spirit felt restless. I knew this wasn't love. It was a situation I had dressed up to look like it. The conviction hit hardest on a Sunday morning in church.

I remember standing during worship, hands lifted, tears streaming down my face. I whispered under my breath, "God, I can't do this. I don't have the strength to leave. Please help me get out. If this isn't where I'm supposed to be, make a way, anyway."

That was Sunday.

By Friday, He answered.

My phone broke that morning at work. That evening, I went back to the hotel and plugged in the old landline, the one we always kept unplugged because it made that weird noise. A few minutes later, it rang.

A woman's voice asked for him. I handed him the phone, thinking nothing of it. He went still, mumbled, "I'll call you back," and left.

The phone rang again.

I answered.

"Who is this?" she asked.

I told her my name. She immediately remembered me from the party.

"What are you doing there?"

"I live here."

Her breath caught. "That's my man. We just had our daughter."

Before I could even process it, the door flew open. He stormed in, snatched the phone out of the wall, pacing like a man possessed. "I'm tired of living a lie," he said. "I'm going back to her."

It was like the air left the room. I felt heat crawl up my face, a mix of shock, confusion, and humiliation. I grabbed an empty duffel bag and threw it, not at him, just away, because the pain needed somewhere to go.

That sound flipped a switch in him. He lunged toward me, eyes wild. His voice thundered, "Don't you ever play with me! Don't you ever play with me!"

Both his hands were around my throat, squeezing with all his strength. I looked up at him and looked into his eyes. He was gone. Something else had taken over. Black spots started forming in my vision. I couldn't breathe. All I could hear was my heartbeat hammering in my ears and his words echoing over and over.

My mind went still. I knew I was going to die that night. A part of me gave up and accepted it. I began to pray, repenting of my sins and saying the Lord's Prayer in my head.

Somewhere deep inside, something rose. I fought back with everything in me. I started punching him in his head with every piece of strength I had left. He had to let me go. I could breathe again. The air came in sharp, painful gasps.

He stared at me, blank, like he didn't even know what had happened. Then he turned and walked out.

The police were called, but they didn't know who to believe or who to take to jail. I had gotten some good hits in and left knots on his head. The hotel put us out because they had a zero-tolerance policy for domestic incidents.

I was left standing there, shaking, staring at my reflection in the mirror. My neck was swollen, bruised, and marked by fingerprints that would take days to fade. I wrapped a scarf around my throat and wore it for three days straight, covering the evidence of what loving the wrong man had cost me.

Sometimes God's deliverance doesn't come wrapped in peace, it comes wrapped in exposure.

He left that night, but not alone. She came to pick him up.

A few days later, once I got my phone fixed, she called me. She said she wanted to check on me. She told me I wasn't the first woman he had done this to. That every morning after dropping me off at work in my car, he would go to her house, spend the day with her and their kids, then come back to me like nothing happened.

Then she said something that froze me. "He told me I'm the only woman in his life who makes him be a man. He wants to marry me."

She said it with pride. But I heard pain disguised as victory.

We were both living in delusion. Hers just looked different from mine. She thought she had won; I thought I had lost. The truth was, we were both losing.

After that, everything became clear. I wasn't his peace, his partner, or his priority. I was his convenience, someone to fill a space until he figured out who he really wanted.

That realization hit like cold water. It stripped away the fantasy I had built. I had confused proximity with partnership, and endurance with love.

I wasn't his peace, I was his placeholder.

For the first time, I asked myself the hard questions:

Why was having somebody better than being alone?

Why did I keep trying to earn love from men who didn't even love themselves?

Why did I keep jumping from one broken situation to another, never giving myself time to breathe or heal?

The answer was ugly but honest. If I'm being real, it wasn't them, it was me. I kept searching for validation in people who were never built to hold my value. Every time I thought I had found something new, it was just a different man, same mess, same lesson on repeat.

I want to tell you I learned my lesson right there. But I didn't. A few months later, I met another man. He was smoother, quieter, even more convincing, and somehow, even worse.

Until you heal, your type will always be your trauma in disguise.

And that's how I learned that the do-or-die chick in me had to die first, so the woman I was meant to become could finally live.

When everything fell apart, I didn't have a plan. Just bruises, bills, and a whole lot of broken dreams. I had nowhere to go and no one to call, but even then, God had a way of covering me when I couldn't cover myself.

I found myself standing behind the counter at the hair store one day, trying to smile through the ache, when a woman walked in. We talked for maybe twenty minutes, but somehow she saw something in me worth saving. "You need a place to stay?" she asked, and before I knew it, I was sleeping under her roof.

It still amazes me, the kindness of strangers in a season where I didn't even feel worth helping. Those people didn't owe me a thing. They didn't know me from a can of paint, but they fed me, prayed for me, and gave me a space to rest my head when I couldn't rest my mind.

Eventually, her mother came back to town, and she needed the room I had been staying in. She handed me a handful of scrap gold and said, "Sell this and get you a fresh start." I did. I sold it, took the cash, and walked straight to an apartment office. Somehow, by the grace of God, I got approved. A place that was mine, a tiny studio that felt like a mansion to me.

You would think that moment of grace would have been my wake-up call that I would have paused, healed, learned, and grown. But I didn't. I still craved love more than I craved wisdom. And because I hadn't learned my lesson, I found myself opening the door to another story, one that would test me in ways I wasn't ready for.

3

Catching L's and Lessons

Some lessons don't come from classrooms. They come from heartbreak.

The lights in that Jacksonville nightclub were hot and bright, bouncing off the gold shimmer on my skin. The mic was warm in my hand, and the crowd was moving with me, heads nodding, fingers snapping, somebody in the back shouting, "Sing it, girl!" That stage was my safe place. My escape. My reminder that even when life was messy, I still had something beautiful inside of me.

When I walked off stage that night, I felt good and light. That's when I saw him. Smooth, confident, standing by the bar like he owned the room. He said he was a producer, told me he loved my sound, and wanted to work with me. He had that calm kind of energy that made you listen. I thought, finally, somebody who gets it.

We set up a time to meet. He said he was staying with his aunt and uncle, so I met him at their apartment. He had beats ready, real music, polished and professional. I was impressed. I picked out a few tracks, and within two days, I had songs written. I was excited. It felt like something big might be about to happen.

I started picking him up so we could record at my place, a small studio apartment that I had worked hard for. He would come over, we would work on music for hours, and I would drop him off. Then one day, he said his aunt and uncle were moving and asked if he could crash on my couch for a week or two. He was helping me with my dream, so I said yes.

That's how it started. First, the couch. Then, of course, the bed.

At first, he was charming, attentive, and thoughtful. He made me laugh and made me feel safe, or at least that's what I thought safety felt like. But slowly, things shifted. The compliments turned into comparisons. The love started to feel like control.

I'll never forget when he brought me cellulite cream. He handed it to me with a smile, like he was doing me a favor. And he would joke that when I sat down next to him, the couch would shake, acting like it was funny. But it wasn't. Those jokes stuck. They chipped away at my confidence until I started wondering if maybe he was right.

The crazy part is, I never judged him. He hid so much from me, things about his life, his past, even parts of himself he was insecure about. But I loved him anyway. I saw the man, not the flaws. Meanwhile, he was doing everything he could to make me doubt myself.

And the audacity of it all, this man had no job. He was living off unemployment, talking about how he was focusing on music. I was the one clocking in every morning, standing on my feet all day at that beauty-supply store for seven twenty-five an hour, trying to keep us both afloat.

One day during an argument, he looked me dead in my face and called me a bald-head, lazy b***.

Lazy.

Me.

The same woman getting up early, pulling double shifts, making sure the bills were paid while he sat home chasing beats. I remember just standing there, stunned, not even sure what hurt worse, the insult or the irony.

Now listen, my mouth back then wasn't saved or sanctified by any means. I could be slick when I needed to be. My tongue was my shield. I could go toe to toe with the best of them, and I would say some things I can't even repeat now. But it was always after being provoked. That was my defense mechanism; it hurt me, and I would hurt you faster. If you went low, I would go lower to prove you couldn't break me.

But deep down, I wasn't trying to win the argument. I was trying not to lose myself.

Then came Halloween. I found out I was pregnant. I told him that night, and he smiled, said everything was going to be fine. The next day was rent day. He told me to relax and said he would take the money to the office for me. Normally, I would never let anyone else handle that, but he was my man and about to be the father of my child. I trusted him.

He took the envelope with both our halves inside, kissed me on my forehead, and said, "I got it."

He came back later, like everything was normal. Ate dinner. Watched TV. Slept beside me. I didn't think twice.

A few weeks later, a notice was taped to my door. Rent unpaid.

I remember standing there with that paper in my hand, stomach turning. I went to the office to find out what was going on, and he even came with me, acting confused and pretending to check it with me. He played the role so well that I believed him.

About two weeks went by, and he said he was going to New York to work on some music and make quick money. He promised he would send something back so we could catch up. At that point, I was one month pregnant and still trying to believe he meant well.

At first, he called every day, checking on me, asking how I felt, telling me about the studio. It wasn't much, but those calls helped me breathe. Every time he called, it gave me just enough hope to believe he had my back. Then the calls got shorter. Then they stopped coming every day. It didn't click until months later that he had taken the rent money. What a low-down thing to do.

By the time I was four, maybe five months pregnant, I hadn't seen a dime from him. Not one. That's when I started calling him, asking what was going on, telling him I needed help. That's when his whole tone changed. He started saying things like, "Every time you call me, you're complaining," and "I got stuff going on here too."

That's when I realized his concern had an expiration date.

I can still remember hanging up that phone one night and just staring at it, like maybe if I looked long enough, he would call back and say he didn't mean it. He never did.

Somehow, by the grace of God, I managed to catch up on the rent. I don't remember how. Maybe somebody helped me, maybe it was a small miracle, but I got it done. Still, I was broke, scared, and pregnant.

He left me in a hole and didn't look back.

By the time I hit five months, my body started betraying me. It was like everything that had been holding me together just gave out at once. I got so weak that even standing too long felt like a battle. Working wasn't an option anymore. My body decided for me.

I didn't have family in Jacksonville, and the ones who loved me most were back home. I was too ashamed to go home to my family, even though I knew they would have welcomed me with open arms. But I was too embarrassed to call. Pride can be a prison. I didn't want to have to explain how I had let a man use me, break me, and leave me holding the bag. So I stayed silent. I stayed small.

Months passed with no word from him. That relationship taught me the difference between love and attachment, between a partner and a parasite. I caught L's, no doubt, losses, lies, and lessons. But I also caught something else: a glimpse of my own strength.

He walked away, but I stayed. Stayed surviving. Stayed becoming.

And the next chapter? That's when the real fight began, because the day I gave birth, I had to drive myself to the hospital and do it all alone. I wasn't supposed to do it alone. Someone had promised to take me and be there with me. She was a no-call, no-show. By the time I realized she wasn't coming, frustration set in. I was too hurt and too tired to reach out to anyone else. My mom would have been there in a heartbeat. She was planning to come once we went home so she could help me with postpartum care.

I got behind the wheel, belly heavy, heart pounding, praying I could make it. The drive to the hospital felt endless. I don't think I have ever felt that kind of silence before. It wasn't just quiet, it was hollow. It was the kind of quiet that forces you to face yourself. That was the loneliest drive of my life. But somewhere between those stoplights and that hospital entrance, something inside me shifted.

Because in that moment, I realized I wasn't just carrying a baby. I was carrying the weight of everything I had survived, and somehow, I was still moving. Still breathing. Still becoming. That drive wasn't just the road to the hospital. It was the road to me.

Labor was only six hours. I remember rocking through the pain and praying. When my son was born, I was surprised. His skin was pale, his hair was soft and blonde like sunlight, and his piercing blue eyes. I didn't understand at first, but he was beautiful. To me, he was perfect. Mine. It made every moment worth it. I stared into his eyes, and I knew I would do anything for him. That was a love I had never felt before.

In the days that followed, a few people came bearing gifts and checking on me. Each visit meant the world to me.

I was still in the hospital when my phone rang. It was him. Somehow, someone told him I had the baby. After all that silence, now he wanted to apologize. He said he was sorry for everything he put me through, sorry for how he treated me. He asked for a picture of the baby, and then he said four words that sent a shock through my whole body.

"Whose baby is that?"

Let's get this straight. We lived together. You stole my rent. You abandoned me while I was pregnant. And now you dare to question if the child was yours.

Disgust doesn't even begin to cover what I felt in that moment. I didn't have the energy to argue or read him his rights. I was done. I knew the truth, and deep down, he knew it too.

4

Same Story Different Face

The first two weeks were a blur. I didn't know what I was doing. I didn't even know you were supposed to heat the baby's milk. I was figuring it out as I went. I was determined to get it right. I met with specialists, and that's when I learned that my son was going to need extra care and attention. There would be vision specialists, early interventions, and things I had to stay on top of to make sure he had everything he needed to thrive.

I had a moment with God. I remember sitting on the edge of the bed, holding my baby, and asking Him, "Why me? Why would you give me a baby who needs so much when I barely have enough for myself?"

I wasn't angry, just scared. I didn't feel equipped. I didn't feel qualified. I wondered why He didn't give my son to a two-parent home, to somebody with money, someone who could provide more. It wasn't that I saw my son as a burden. It was the opposite. I saw him as a gift, so I didn't want to fail him.

After the series of appointments, my mother had enough. She put her foot down and said, "I'm coming to get you and my grandbaby," and I knew there was no more fighting it. Two weeks after I had my son, I packed up everything and went back home to my mama's house. I needed help. I needed support. I needed somebody to hold me up while I tried to hold my life together. For a while, that's exactly what I did.

When I moved back to North Carolina, I started to feel like life was finally giving me a second chance. I was rebuilding, slowly but surely, finding my rhythm as a mom, getting back on my feet, and rediscovering pieces of myself I had lost along the way.

Then, out of nowhere, I ran into someone familiar.

We had known each other for years, grew up in the same area, and knew each other's families. He was easy to talk to because there was history there, familiarity. And to top it off, he did music too. Music had always been my outlet, my therapy before I even knew what therapy was, so we started working together. I was writing again, pouring my pain into lyrics, trying to heal through melody. But music wasn't the only thing that connected us.

One thing led to another, and before long, we were together. It felt safe at first. Comfortable. Like, maybe this time I had found someone who really understood me.

About three months in, I started going back to church. Something in me was stirring again. I rededicated my life to Christ and started showing up faithfully. Every service felt like another piece of me being restored. I was hopeful. I was healing. I finally felt like I was getting somewhere. And then, bam.

I found out I was pregnant again. My baby boy was only four months old.

When I saw those two lines on the test, I just sat there in silence. My stomach dropped. I wasn't even shocked at first, just numb. Then it hit me, and I remember whispering,
 "God... not again."

I felt like a failure. I had just started getting myself together, just started going back to church, feeling like I was finally turning things around. I had made peace with my past and told myself I was doing better, and then this. I was so disappointed in myself. I didn't even want to face anyone, especially not my church family. I could already hear the whispers, the questions, the looks.

I remember sitting there, crying, feeling like I had let God down, my mama down, and even myself down. I kept thinking, You were supposed to do better this time. You were supposed to know better. I carried shame like it was part of my wardrobe. But underneath the shame, there was still this small flicker of something else. It was love. Because no matter how disappointed I was, I already loved that little life growing inside me. I didn't know how I was going to make it work, but I knew I would.

It broke my heart to realize I was about to raise another child on my own, but I didn't have the luxury of falling apart. I had a son depending on me.

My mom had a hard time with me during that season, but not in the way most would think. She wasn't angry; she was concerned. She has always been the kind of woman who says what she means and means what she says. Her love has never been soft, but it has always been real.

I'll never forget the day she sat me down. She looked me straight in the eye and said, "Now this is number two. How many times are you going to do this? You know you have a call on your life. You have a destiny. I'm not judging you, but I need you to see what's happening. These choices are slowing you down. You just had a baby, and now another one is on the way. This isn't about shame, it's about purpose."

She wasn't calling my children a mistake. She was proud of them and proud of me for being their mother. But she also knew that raising them without a stable partner would make the journey harder. She wanted me to think long-term, not just emotionally. And she was right. She was trying to protect me from struggle, from cycles, from myself.

Her words didn't come from disappointment. They came from love, from a woman who had seen enough life to know that just getting by would never be enough for the kind of purpose she knew God had placed in me, on me, and in the daughter I was carrying.

Those early years were some of the hardest of my life. Two children under two was like having twins. Everywhere I went, I was lugging car seats, diaper bags, and exhaustion. One baby on my hip, the other in a carrier. I don't think I ever sat still for more than five minutes.

On top of that, there were the appointments, visual specialists, early intervention programs, follow-ups, and evaluations. My days revolved around schedules and checklists. I wanted to give my babies everything, but there were nights I would sit crying quietly so I wouldn't wake them.

It wasn't that I didn't love being their mother, I didn't know how to be everything they needed while I was still trying to figure out who I was.

But I'll never forget bringing them to church. I would walk in, one on my hip and one in a stroller, trying to hold it all together. One of the church mothers would look at me and smile with a knowing in her eyes. She would stop me after service and say, "Baby, it won't be like this always. You're doing good. Just keep pushing." She would tell me about her own days of raising babies alone and how, somehow, God always made a way.

She reminded me to cherish those moments, the sleepless nights, the bottles, the cries, because the days are long, but the years are short. And even though I was tired, her words gave me strength. It was like God used that woman as a messenger, reminding me that I wasn't forgotten, that I was seen.

Yes, after a while, I started to chill out. Life began to find its rhythm again. My babies were growing, I was healing little by little, and things weren't as heavy as they once were. But even in that season of peace, there was still a part of me that ached, the part that wanted my children to have the kind of stability I grew up with.

I had a father in the home. He cared for us. He provided, protected, and made sure our needs were met. I thank God for that foundation because it showed me what love, presence, and responsibility were supposed to look like. That's what I wanted for my children: that steady covering, a feeling of safety, a reminder that they were loved and seen by both parents.

Every birthday party, every Sunday morning at church, every night, I felt the absence. Not because I wasn't enough for them, but because I wanted them to have everything. I told myself I was content, but deep down, I still longed for family. For stability. For the picture I had always imagined.

And that desire, as pure as it was, made me vulnerable. Because when he came along, the one who showed interest in not just me but my children, I convinced myself he was the answer to my prayers. He was kind to them, he treated them well, and in my heart, I thought, Finally. Finally, a father figure. Finally, the two-parent home I had always dreamed of. This was my shot at redemption.

I also felt like my options were limited. I had two little ones, and in my mind, that meant baggage. I didn't think men would want to deal with that. So when someone, anyone, showed me interest, I held onto it tighter than I should have.

He came into my life right when I was trying to prove I had it all together. I had two little ones, a new place, and a plan to finally get it right. I wasn't looking for a fairytale. I just wanted help, partnership, to be loved, and somebody to make life feel lighter. And he played the part perfectly. He said all the right things, made all the right promises. The way he looked at me, the way he showed up, felt like the kind of love I had been waiting for.

But looking back now, I realize it wasn't love knocking at my door. It was another lesson dressed like it.

I married this lesson.

5

Loving Him Almost Killed Me

It still crosses my mind sometimes
"I'm sorry for choking you. I just wanted you to shut up."

That should have been my cue to leave.

I never saw it coming. Not from him. Not from someone I had stood before God and family and vowed to love, honor, and build a life with. It happened within the first few months of our marriage. Still in that space where you are supposed to be figuring things out, learning from each other, building routines, adjusting. The newlywed phase.

I never thought I would find myself in that situation again.

I had already been there once. A few years earlier, I was in a short-lived relationship with someone who crossed that line. He choked me. And I walked away. No questions. No chances. No explanations. I left and never looked back. So in my mind, that chapter was closed. I had survived it. I had grown past it. I had made a promise to myself that I would never allow that kind of harm again.

So when it happened in my marriage with someone I loved, trusted, and vowed my life to, it didn't just hurt. It shattered something in me.

This wasn't a boyfriend I barely knew. I remember the moment like it split something inside me. The yelling started, then the name-calling. Then suddenly it escalated. Hands were no longer just for holding. The person I loved, the person I trusted to cover me, put his hands on me. And just like that, the atmosphere shifted from love to fear from sacred to unsafe.

I froze. Not because I was weak, but because I was stunned. I couldn't wrap my mind around it. It was like I left my body for a moment, trying to convince myself it didn't happen. Trying to find a version of the story that made it makes sense. But there was no editing this. No sugarcoating it.

The man I married, the man I believed in, hurt me.

I was sure that it was just an isolated incident. He was overwhelmed and upset. So I stayed. I felt obligated to stay. I thought being a wife meant being his ride-or-die, no matter what.

And then it happened again.

But I stayed. He needed my love to fix him. Who would he have if I walked away? I thought maybe, if I prayed harder, stayed quieter, did everything right, and avoided provoking him, things would get better.

I believed that if I loved enough, endured enough, showed enough grace, I could love the anger out of him. But I couldn't. No amount of love could reach the broken parts of him. And my silence only made the violence louder. What I didn't realize then was that I was shrinking. Fading. Piece by piece, I was disappearing, trying to save him while losing myself.

His abuse wasn't just emotional. It was physical. Violent. Terrifying. Sometimes I felt like a rag doll the way he would sling me around the room. I just knew one day he would get hold of me, and that would be it. That would be my last day. My last breath. My last moment. And still, I stayed.

It was like something else would take over him, like he wasn't even human anymore. His eyes would go blank, his voice would change, and suddenly, he would have this unnatural strength. One day, he got so mad that he picked up the refrigerator and slammed it down. A whole refrigerator. I stood there frozen, watching it crash to the floor, relieved it wasn't me, thinking, This can't be real. This has to be a movie. But it wasn't. It was my life.

One night, I was so afraid that I grabbed my babies and rushed into the bedroom, pushed a dresser in front of the door to keep him from getting in. My hands trembled as I held them close, trying to calm their tears while hiding my own fear. He beat on the door a few times, then finally gave up and went to bed. He was so angry. So out of control. And yet somehow, I still thought that if I could change, things would be okay.

It was like night and day. When he wanted to be thoughtful, he went all out.

His marriage proposal? Epic.
Our first Valentine's Day? Straight out of a movie.

He filled the dining room with balloons and flowers, showered me with my favorite gifts, and made me feel like the most loved woman in the world. In public, he was proud to have me on his arm. He showed me off, raved about me, told everyone how lucky he was. And in those moments, I believed it. I felt seen. Cherished. Protected.

That's the husband I wanted all the time. That version of him who made me feel safe and adored was the one I kept holding onto. Hoping he would stay. Praying he would come back.

When we were in pre-marital counselling, he sold the pastor and me a pipe dream. He said all the right things, wore all the right masks. And for a moment, I believed him. We both did. But it was all a performance, a carefully crafted illusion. He wasn't there to love me; he was there to hide.

Thirty days. It took thirty days, and the mask came off. Lies began to surface, one after the other. Who did I marry? This wasn't the man I prayed for. This wasn't the man who whispered promises in my ear, who stood before God with tears in his eyes, pledging to protect and love me. This was someone different, manipulative, defensive, dishonest.

And the scariest part? I was warned.

The morning before he proposed to me, I had a dream. I'll never forget it. I woke up around five in the morning, heart pounding, spirit uneasy. And in that dream, I heard God clearly, more clearly than I had in a long time. He said, "The counterfeit comes before the blessing." Those were His exact words.

And I knew they weren't random. I knew it was Him. But I misinterpreted it, or maybe I didn't. Maybe I didn't want to hear what He was actually saying. Because when you're tired, when you've already been through so much, when you're craving stability and covering and partnership, you start making almost look like enough.

I was a single mom. Two babies under three. Unmarried. Trying to find my footing while serving in ministry, while carrying dreams, while battling shame. And somewhere inside, I started to believe that if I ever wanted to be fully accepted, especially in the church, I needed a husband.

So I convinced myself that maybe I could make it work. That I could fix it, pray through it, love him into being the right one.

He told me. He told me before the ring, before the vows, before the heartbreak. And I ignored Him.

I loved being a wife, even though most days it felt like I didn't have a husband.

He told us that he didn't want me to work. At first, it sounded like care. Like protection. Like love. But it wasn't long before I realized what it really was: control. Without a job or the ability to contribute financially, I had no say in anything.

He picked the house we moved into.
 He bought the groceries I had to cook.
 He gave me a forty-dollar allowance when he got paid, as if I were a child and not his wife.

I was living, but not alive.

He constantly reminded me that he "took me and my two kids in," as if we were strays he'd rescued from the street as if I should be grateful. As if gratitude meant blind obedience.

I didn't know when the bills were due or where to pay them. He said it wasn't my place to know. When the landlord came around, he would tell me to take the kids inside. There were times the water was cut off, and I had no idea why. The lights would go out, and I would better not have said a word.

He had the only car, and instead of letting me drop him off so I could get out of the house, he said he didn't feel like walking across campus.

So I stayed home. Trapped. The walls felt like they were caving in. It seemed like he just wanted me in the house. Isolated and alone.

My only outlet was church on Sundays and Bible study during the week. That was my breath of air. My moment of peace.

I promised myself I would never let another man handle me that way again, like I was less than, just because I didn't bring in a paycheck. From that moment on, I made sure I had a side hustle, something of my own. I didn't care if it was small; it was mine.

Where we should have been a team, it felt like we were on opposite sides. He didn't want a partner. He wanted the upper hand.

But guess what?

God flipped the switch almost instantly. His car got repossessed... and not long after, I was blessed with one. And even though he had been stingy, I wasn't. Sometimes I let him use the car. Sometimes I drove him where he needed to go. I wasn't trying to throw anything in his face. I was trying to help.

I picked up a side hustle, started making a little money, and when there was a lack, I filled in the gaps. I did my best to be a helpmeet. I even got a few food stamps so I could buy the groceries I wanted. But even then, I was thoughtful. I made sure to get what he liked, too. I always considered him.

The truth is, I was hardly considered unless he felt like it.

And I meant it when I said: I will never again let someone have that kind of control over me just because they make the money. My spirit was already bruised. While I was trying to rise, to be supportive, to still hold it all together... he kept drifting farther away.

He got home at five forty-five every Monday through Friday. He didn't like his food piping hot, so I timed it perfectly every day like clockwork. He would walk in, sit down, eat, and be out the door by six fifteen. Gone until ten or eleven at night. I got used to being married but feeling single.

I brought it up once. Just once.
 Let's say... after that, he came and went as he pleased.

I was in a very dark place. Only a few people knew how bad it really was. On the outside, I smiled. I functioned. I survived. But inside, I was unravelling. The emotional rollercoasters were unbearable. I started having anxiety attacks, and my hands would shake uncontrollably. I couldn't sleep. I couldn't breathe. I felt like I was losing my mind.

Eventually, I was diagnosed with PTSD and put on antidepressants. I had become a shell of the woman I once was.

I used to be a fireball, bold, outspoken, unshakable.
 I stood up for myself. I knew who I was.

But over time, I went quiet. Not because I had nothing to say, but because I was trying to keep the peace.

My children still remember, clear as day, him putting his hands on me. And that's what haunts me the most. Not just what I endured, but what I exposed them to. What kind of mother was I? I remember crying to my three-year-old, apologizing for the life I had brought him into. And my sweet baby looked up at me and said, "Pray, Mama. You've got to pray."

That broke me. Shattered me.

He never hurt my kids, thankfully. But they saw too much. Felt too much.

The gaslighting was relentless. Everything, absolutely everything, was somehow my fault. And the worst part? I believed him. I started to question my own memory, my own instincts, my own reality. That kind of manipulation doesn't just confuse you, it erases you, piece by piece.

We were separated more than we were together. I got put out of the house for months at a time. He would throw the children's clothes and toys out in the front yard, then do the same with mine. I would stay with my grandma, and then he would call, saying he wanted his family back. I don't know if he didn't want to be alone in the house or if he was worried about who I was with and where I was going. It couldn't have been because he missed me. After all, he hardly paid me any attention unless he was mad about something.

Full of delusion, I went back time after time.
The last time I returned, he put me in the guest bedroom
like I had to earn my way back into the main bedroom.
Like I was a visitor in my own marriage.
I look back at those times, and I can't believe I tolerated
that kind of mistreatment. But I did. I took my vows
seriously because I believed in marriage. Because I
wanted to make it work.
But one day, a light bulb went off.

I finally woke up. I filed for divorce. I had to end the cycle.
Because if I hadn't, we would still be married today,
separated eight months of the year, sleeping in separate
rooms, walking on eggshells, and on the verge of a
nervous breakdown.

The truth is, I wasn't what he wanted, and I finally
realized I didn't have to keep proving my worth to
someone who couldn't see it. So I let go.

He used to say, "I should've left you at your grandma's
house."
 And honestly? He was right.

He should never have come into my life.
 All he did was leave chaos behind.

He didn't build anything. He only tore things down.
 What he touched, he damaged.
 What he promised, he destroyed.

"You don't owe anyone you're healing. Leaving is proof you finally chose yourself."

There were two times. Not once, but twice that he came back.

The same man who bruised me, belittled me, and broke me down in every way you can break a person. The same man who watched me cry myself to sleep in silence because I was too afraid to make a sound. The same man who held my finances hostage, twisted my mind, and made me question the worth God had stamped on me from birth. The same one who hurt me, then blamed me for bleeding.

He came back. And you want to know what he said?

He said, "You were too good for me."
He said, "I didn't deserve somebody like you."

He called me after the damage, after I had begun the hard work of rebuilding what he tried to destroy, and he said, "Your heart is pure. You've always been kind to me even when I mistreated you. Even when I did the unimaginable, even when I brought shame to your name, you never stopped being kind."

He was right. I did love him fiercely, sacrificially, and with my whole soul. But I also loved him to my own detriment. I loved him when he made me feel invisible. I stayed loyal when he gave me every reason to run. I defended him in public while bleeding in private. I gave chances that weren't earned, forgiveness that was never honored, and grace that he never reciprocated.

And if I'm being real, even after that first call, I was still scared of him. Not just emotionally, but physically. The kind of fear that sits in your chest and doesn't leave easily. I would see him around town sometimes, and every single time, my heart would drop straight to my stomach. I would freeze. My breath would catch. I would speak quick and keep it short, then walk off before my voice could shake.

He didn't have to raise his hand again for me to remember. My body already knew what that kind of danger felt like. I was polite out of survival, not softness. That fear lived in me longer than the relationship did.

Years later, after life had moved on, he reached out again. This time through Facebook. This time, not just with remorse but with torment. He said he was tortured that he couldn't sleep at night. That the way he treated me haunted him. That was the way he mishandled me followed him like a ghost. He needed to know I forgave him.

I read it. Not for closure. But for confirmation.

I didn't need revenge. I didn't need him to suffer. I didn't need validation. I realized I was never hard to love. I just gave my love to someone who didn't know what to do with it.

When he said those words, I didn't feel vindicated, I felt seen by God. It was like heaven whispered, "Now you can stop carrying what I already freed you from." His apology didn't heal me; God had already done that. His words were only the echo of a lesson I had already learned in secret, that I was never the broken one. I wasn't hard to love; I just gave my love to someone who couldn't handle it.

And once that truth settled in, the noise stopped.
 The calls stopped.
 The chaos stopped.

Life got quite painfully quiet.

That's when God started speaking the loudest, right there in the silence I used to hate.

Sometimes God clears the room so you can finally hear Him.

SECTION TWO

THE HEALING I DIDN'T KNOW I NEEDED

6

Alone, But Not Abandoned

I used to wonder why God would let me face some of the hardest seasons of my life by myself. Why did I have to walk through heartbreak, sickness, and loss with nobody in sight? It never made sense to me back then. I couldn't understand why the same people I had prayed for, showed up for, encouraged, and carried, couldn't seem to do the same for me when it was my turn to need help.

It was sobering to realize that some people dropped me because I wasn't useful to them anymore. Others let go because the weight of my situation was too heavy for them to carry. Either way, it hurt. And for a long time, I took it personal. I kept replaying the names, the moments, the conversations. But eventually, I realized it wasn't about punishment; it was about purpose. Those seasons were designed to strip away everything and everyone that distracted me from hearing God clearly.

At first, it felt cruel, as if He were punishing me. But really, He was protecting me. He needed the noise to stop so He could get my attention. Because the truth is, I had become addicted to motion. I was always doing for people, doing for love, doing to be seen, doing to be needed. I didn't know how to just be. So he sat me down. And when I say sat me down, I mean He allowed back-to-back seasons that forced me to be still. There was no more performing. No more pretending. Just me, Him, and the silence.

It was in that silence that I heard Him the loudest. When I couldn't call anybody else, I learned how to call on Him for real. In those months of stillness, those long, quiet days where I felt forgotten, He reminded me who I was. I thought the solitude was punishment, but it was surgery. He was cutting out everything in me that sought validation from broken places. The people pleasing. The need to be seen. The overextending. All of it had to die there.

And it did. Slowly, painfully, but completely.

Those seasons taught me that not every loss is abandonment. Some are alignment. Some people have to leave so God can fill the space they occupy. And now, when I look back, I see that being alone wasn't my breaking; it was my becoming.

Because even now, as I walk through yet another season, I don't see it the same. I don't see the isolation as rejection anymore. I see it as refinement. I see it as evidence that He still has more work to do in me. And this time, instead of fighting the silence, I've learned to rest in it.

These days, peace doesn't look like perfection. It looks like quiet mornings with no rush, deep breaths without guilt, and learning how to let people show up for me instead of always showing up for everyone else. It looks like letting go without resentment, praying without panic, and finally trusting that I don't have to prove I'm worthy of love.

I've learned that healing isn't loud. It's layered. It's the unseen rewiring that happens after the breakdown. It's the soft voice that says, "You're safe now." And I finally believe it.

Because even when I thought I was alone, I was surrounded. Even when I was stripped, I was being shaped. And even now, in this new season, I can see how every quiet place was actually a sacred place.

SECTION THREE

THE BECOMING

7

I'm Not Too Much I'm an acquired taste

The quiet didn't just heal me, it introduced me to me. In the stillness, I finally heard my own voice without the noise of opinions, obligations, or expectations. I realized that God hadn't abandoned me at all; He was isolating me to refine me. That season wasn't punishment; it was preparation.

But something shifted in that solitude. The loneliness that once felt like rejection began to feel like revelation. I started seeing who I truly was beyond who people said I should be. And for the first time in a long time, I didn't feel the urge to prove myself. I just wanted to be myself.

That's where I learned one of the hardest truths: I was never too much; I was just around people who wanted less.

The silence taught me that my voice was never the problem; it was just echoing in the wrong rooms.

For so long, I thought being "too much" was a flaw. Too emotional. Too passionate. Too opinionated. Too ambitious. Too everything. I tried to tone myself down, dress myself down, and water myself down so other people could swallow me more easily. But all that did was make me disappear in rooms I was meant to dominate.

Those quiet months alone with God stripped away my need for applause. I learned that validation doesn't sound like clapping, it sounds like peace. I realized that being misunderstood doesn't mean you're wrong; it just means you're different.

Some people loved the soft parts of me, but couldn't handle the strong ones. Others admired my resilience but were intimidated by my light. I used to take that personally. Now I understand it's not rejection; it's refinement.

Because I was never created to be easily consumed, I was created to be savored, to be understood, not just seen. That's why I call myself an acquired taste. I'm not for everybody, and that's okay.

I've learned that when you start walking in your full truth, the wrong people will quietly exit, and the right ones will recognize your frequency and find you. I no longer chase rooms I've outgrown or relationships that require me to shrink.

I didn't even realize how much I used to shrink until I stopped doing it. The first time I said "no" without overexplaining, it felt like freedom. The first time I walked into a room without trying to make everyone comfortable with my presence, it felt like power. I started showing up as myself, all of me, no matter who was in the room.

My posture changed. My tone changed. Even my silence started speaking differently. I no longer needed to defend my choices or soften my opinions to make others feel secure. I stopped performing. I stopped auditioning for love, friendship, and belonging.

The more I embraced who I was, the more peace I felt. I didn't have to chase opportunities; they started finding me. My energy became magnetic because it was finally real.

I started setting boundaries without guilt. I stopped overexplaining my no's and stopped apologizing for my yes's. I used to think confidence was loud, but I learned it's actually quiet. It's walking into a room knowing you belong there, even if nobody claps.

And the truth is, once you start operating in your authenticity, you see everything differently: relationships, friendships, business, even faith. I realized that when God said He made me in His image, He didn't mean I had to dim the parts of me that made others uncomfortable. He meant I was designed with intention, and intention doesn't apologize for existing.

Now, I walk differently. I speak differently. I see myself differently. I no longer strive to be digestible. I aim to be authentic. Because the woman I am becoming doesn't beg for space, she creates it.

I'm not "too much." I'm just more than they were prepared for.

Peace found me when I stopped trying to earn it. I don't wrestle for belonging anymore. I show up as myself, knowing that who I am is already enough. The quiet taught me that wholeness isn't about being liked, it's about being free. I don't need the world to approve of me to know I'm valuable. I've finally accepted that I'm not for everybody, but I am absolutely for me.

And that's the kind of freedom I refuse to lose again.

Coming out of that season of stillness, I realized something deeper. I wasn't misunderstood because I was too much. I was misunderstood because I was multi-layered. I had spent years apologizing for the way God made me, trying to explain why I had so many gifts, so many interests, so many dreams that never seemed to fit neatly in one box.

But I finally understood that boxes were never meant for builders. And I was born to build.

That revelation ushered me into my next chapter, because once I stopped trying to shrink my capacity, I had to learn to manage it.

8

You Can't Teach Me How to Be Me

For most of my life, I've been good at a lot. Creative. Capable. Gifted in more ways than I could count. But somewhere along the way, I started feeling like being multitalented was a problem. Like I was doing too much. Like I needed to sit down and pick one.

People made me feel like my versatility made me scattered. But the truth is, God made me layered on purpose. I'm not confused. I'm called. And the beauty of being multi-gifted is knowing that not every gift is meant for every season. Some things are for right now. Some things are for what's next. And some things were never meant for a stage; they were meant to grow me in secret.

I didn't always have the discernment to know the difference.

But now I ask God,

"What is this season pulling on in me?"

"What makes sense right now?"

"What will bring peace, not just pressure?"

"What will bear fruit, not just force me to perform?"

63

And sometimes that answer hurts. Because it means letting go of things I used to love, things that once lit me up but now wear me out. Other times, it means walking into something brand new, unfamiliar, and uncomfortable, which makes me second-guess everything.

But I've learned this: if I'm constantly forcing it, if frustration starts speaking louder than passion, that isn't growth. That's a red flag. That's God telling me to pause. To pivot. To get still and realign.

"You're not confused, you're just no longer available for counterfeit definitions."

But I didn't always listen. There were years when I stayed in things way too long. I kept pushing when I should have paused. I kept striving when I should have surrendered.

I was drained, disconnected, and depleted. Not because I wasn't gifted, but because I was out of alignment. I was following people's opinions instead of God's instructions.

People had their own blueprint for my life. They liked the version of me that was dependable, predictable, and available. The one who always showed up, stayed loyal, and never asked for more. So they boxed me into roles that served them. And I let them.

I didn't speak up. I didn't draw lines. I didn't advocate for the version of me that was evolving. I played it safe, even when my soul was screaming, "We're not meant to stay here."

I stayed out of guilt. I over functioned out of fear. I'm confused about being loyal with being limited.

And then came the opinions.
 "You were so good at that, why stop?"
 "I don't get why you'd walk away from something that was working."

But they weren't the ones pouring from an empty cup. They weren't the ones sacrificing peace to keep up an image. They didn't have to lie in bed at night wondering if they were still being true to themselves.

They weren't living it.
 I was.

You can't teach me how to be me.

And when I finally dared to dream out loud, when I opened my mouth and spoke vision, purpose, and plans that made my heart beat faster, I wasn't met with celebration. I was met with side eyes, smirks, and subtle shade.

"I've never heard of that."
 "Why would you need all of that?"
 "That just sounds like a lot."

Yes, it is a lot.
 Because I am a lot.

I wasn't created to shrink, play small, or dream in pieces. I don't do manageable dreams. I do legacy. I am a builder. A visionary. God gave me eyes to see beyond what's typical and hands to create what has never been done before. And I've learned something important: you cannot expect someone who has never carried your calling to co-sign your vision. They don't get it because it's not meant for them.

People will always try to fit you into the version of yourself that is most comfortable for them. The agreeable version. The quiet version. The one who doesn't ask for too much, take up too much space, or disrupt the norm. But what happens when that version of you starts to suffocate? What happens when you can't keep pretending that the safe version is still enough?

My soul started yelling. Not whispering. Yelling that there was more. And I had to listen. I had to stop asking for permission to grow. I had to stop apologizing for evolving. Because growth isn't always shiny, sometimes it looks like walking away from the very things that once gave you identity. Sometimes it means releasing what used to work, what used to fit, and what used to feel like home.

No one tells you that becoming will break your heart a little. Because even shedding dead weight still feels like a loss. Even letting go of old roles, old dreams, and old identities comes with grief.

But the deeper grief is staying stuck.
 Living small.
 Losing yourself to keep the peace in rooms that no longer reflect who you are becoming.

I had to start telling people, with no guilt in my voice, "I know I used to do that, but that's not my lane anymore."

I've walked away from money. From opportunities. From platforms people would have killed for because they weren't in alignment with where I was headed. They were souvenirs from a version of me that no longer exists.

And that version? She was necessary. She survived some things. She helped me get here. But she cannot take me where I'm going. She is not the author of my next chapter.

Before I could meet the woman I was becoming, I had to lay to rest the one I used to be. The one who performed for belonging, who mistook busyness for purpose, and applause for affirmation. I had to release her with gratitude, thank her for surviving what tried to break me, and still choose to move forward without her.

Because at some point, you stop trying to reinvent yourself and start remembering yourself.

9

I've Been Her All Along

I spent years searching for something I already was, trying to become her.

That woman.

The confident one.

The bold one.

The loved one.

The seen one.

The whole one.

The free one.

But somewhere along the way, I forgot I already was her. She didn't need to be created. She needed to be remembered.

I spent so much of my life editing myself to make other people comfortable, shrinking to be digestible, morphing into whatever version I thought would make people stay. I gave fragments of myself to friendships and relationships that didn't know what to do with my fullness. I dimmed my light to fit into rooms that weren't even built for me.

I told myself I was too loud, too emotional, too ambitious, too sensitive, too bubbly. Too much. When, really, I was just too powerful for people who hadn't yet met themselves.

So I twisted. I bent. I shapeshifted.
 I watered myself down until I could barely taste my own identity.

And for what?

 To keep a seat at tables where I was only tolerated?

 To keep love that came with conditions and expiration dates?

 To be accepted by people who didn't even know how to accept themselves?

It took me years to understand that the real me never disappeared. She was just buried under survival mode, people pleasing, and perfectionism. I called it reinvention, but really, I was in recovery.

Recovery from needing to be chosen.

Recovery from needing to be liked.

Recovery from needing to prove that I was worthy of love, attention, and belonging.

I wasn't lost. I was layered. And God was patiently peeling me back, one painful and beautiful layer at a time.

Somewhere between the breaking and the rebuilding, I realized I no longer wanted to perform for peace. I no longer wanted to earn love that was supposed to be freely given. I no longer wanted to chase validation from myself.

I started seeing the beauty in my own becoming. The woman I prayed for wasn't out there; she was in here.

It took quiet seasons to hear her. It took heartbreaks to uncover her. It took solitude to recognize her reflection. Now I don't apologize for my light anymore.

I don't shrink my laughter, hide my dreams, or dull my sparkle to make other people feel comfortable in their dimness. If my presence feels like too much, maybe they should try expanding their capacity. I used to beg God to make me smaller, quieter, easier to love. Now I thank Him for making me radiant, rare, and unforgettable.

Because every time I thought I had lost myself, He was introducing me to another version of her. The one who is softer but stronger. Wiser but still willing. Open, but no longer available to everyone.

I don't want to prove anything anymore.

I want to be.

Be whole.

Be grounded.

Be seen by me first.

Now, when I walk into a room, I don't shrink to fit it. The room adjusts to me. Because I finally understand I was never too much. I was always just enough for the life God built for me.

When I look back over every version of myself , the broken one, the desperate one, the healing one, and the rising one , I see pieces of her in all of them. Every season was a teacher. Every loss was a mirror. Every heartbreak was holy ground that grew me into the woman I had been searching for all along.

Becoming her was never about changing who I was. It was about coming home to who I have always been. She was the girl who kept loving, even when it hurt. She was there in the woman who walked away when it finally cost too much. She was there in every whispered prayer, every late-night tear, every quiet comeback that nobody clapped for.

And now she is here.

Standing in her truth, standing in her power, standing in her peace.

Not perfect, but present.

Not flawless, but free.

And that, right there, is what becoming looks like.

A LETTER TO THE ONE BECOMING

If you made it this far, take a deep breath because that means you didn't give up on yourself.
 Not when it got ugly. Not when it got lonely. Not when it felt like you lost every version of who you thought you would be. You kept showing up, even when your voice shook. You kept loving, even as you healed. You kept rebuilding, even when your hands were trembling. And that deserves to be celebrated.

If no one has told you lately, I'm proud of you. Not for being perfect, but for being present. For choosing to try again. For doing the hard, holy work of becoming.

Becoming isn't always beautiful. Sometimes it's messy, quiet, and uncomfortable. Sometimes it looks like tears no one sees and prayers that feel unanswered. Sometimes it feels like God is silent when really, He's working on the parts of you that words can't reach.

So if you're in that in-between space right now, the waiting, the wondering, the trying to make sense of it all, hear this:

You are not behind. You're right on schedule.

You are not broken; you are being built.

You are not overlooked; you are being refined.

You are not forgotten; you are being formed.

One day, you'll look back and realize you were becoming the whole time.

You didn't become stronger when people finally saw your worth.

You didn't become wiser when it stopped hurting.

You became when you decided to keep going, even when you didn't know what becoming looked like yet.

Don't rush the process. Don't despise the rebuilding. Every detour, delay, and disappointment is still divine direction.

Keep growing. Keep healing. Keep becoming.

Because the world doesn't need another perfect person, it needs a real one. And that's exactly who you've been becoming all along.

We are becoming, and becoming takes time.

Your Girl,
 Marquita Desire'e

ABOUT THE AUTHOR

Marquita Desire'e is an author, singer, songwriter, speaker, entrepreneur, fashion enthusiast, and creative visionary with a heart for helping people heal, grow, and step into who God created them to be. Through her honest storytelling and transparent truth, she invites readers into the journey of breaking, rebuilding, and rediscovering identity in real time.

She is the founder of The Marquita Desire'e Experience and the host of The Truth Room, where she creates spaces for people from every background to breathe, reflect, and rise. Her work brings together faith, emotional depth, creativity, and lived wisdom, offering encouragement and hope to anyone navigating transition or transformation.

Whether she is writing, designing, singing, speaking, or building community, Marquita leads with authenticity, compassion, and purpose. Her life reflects resilience, restoration, and the courage to begin again.

She continues to walk out her own becoming journey with grace, intention, and God.

www.ingramcontent.com/pod-product-compliance
Lightning Source LLC
Chambersburg PA
CBHW061714120626
46550CB00003B/1211